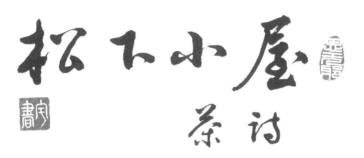

松下小屋

茶诗

# The Hut
## Beneath the Pine

*Tea Poems*
by Daniel Skach-Mills

THE HUT BENEATH THE PINE
Tea Poems
by Daniel Skach-Mills

Copyright © 2011 by Daniel Skach-Mills
skachmills@gmail.com
Designed by Dan Lucas
Illustrations copyright © 2011 by Lu Kesi
Calligraphy copyright © 2011 by Jiyu Yang
Author photograph by Ken Skach-Mills

ISBN 978-0-615-41398-3

# Acknowledgements

I am grateful to editors of publications where some of these works first appeared, perhaps in slightly different versions:

*Windfall: A Journal of Poetry of Place*—"At the Teahouse"

"The Hut Beneath the Pine: Four" which begins, "A person awakened to the Tao is like a good pot of tea ..." first appeared as poem number "Forty-Three" in *The Tao of Now* (Ken Arnold Books, 2008).

With much appreciation to Lu Kesi (Dan Lucas) who generously offered his time and talent designing and illustrating this book; to Dr. Jiyu Yang, whose calligraphy flows like the Tao; and to Margaret Chula, who graciously provided suggestions and comments.

I would also like to thank Aaron Fisher and James Norwood Pratt for their fine books about tea; The Tao of Tea, a purveyor of fine tea in Portland, Oregon; and Teance teahouse (Berkeley, California) for their exquisite DVD, *The Renaissance of Tea*.

And with gratitude for Stephen Mitchell's, *The Second Book of the Tao*, and Lois Baker's, *Fragrant Mountain: Twenty-Four Early Poems of Fan Chengda*.

To the staff at
*The Tower of Cosmic Reflections* teahouse,
Lan Su Chinese Garden—Portland, Oregon,
and to all those who make the gift
of the Garden possible.

And in fond memory of Harry,
who introduced me to my first cup
of Lapsang Souchong.

# Contents

Introduction  1

The Teahouse In Spring  5

The Hut Beneath The Pine  7

Synesthesia  45

Tea Trio  47

Cha Tao  55

Watching An Old Monk Drink Tea  57

On Retreat  59

At The Hermitage  61

Observing An Elderly Couple Sipping Tea
      At A Table Outside The Teahouse  63

At The Pavilion For Washing Away Thoughts  65

At The Teahouse  67

Now That I Realize Inner And Outer Are One  69

Glossary/Notes  71

About The Author  75

"Tea is a place to escape to when you cannot ease your cares in the mountains. Tea is the hut beneath the pine in the midst of the city."

— *Toyohara Sumiaki*

Tao is the flow of nature
pouring into and out of form.
Tea is the flow of nature
pouring into and out of your cup.

Tea is the Tao in disguise.
Tao is what gives rise
to everything—drink and drinker,
the cup and the cup's emptiness.

Straining thoughts from your mind
and words from your tongue,
can you savor the One Taste?

— *Daniel Skach-Mills*

# Introduction

I have been leading tours at Lan Su Chinese Garden in Portland, Oregon since 2005. At the end of each tour I point to the Garden teahouse, *The Tower of Cosmic Reflections*, and say to the group, "in the Taoist world view, tea is the Tao in disguise."

*Tao is the flow of nature pouring into and out of form.* •
*Tea is the flow of nature pouring into and out of your cup.*

Usually, more than a few smile knowingly and nod. And for a moment there is a shared recognition, a connection between us that tea has brewed up and served.

This connection is not to be taken lightly. Most people feel a pervasive *disconnection* from life, despite our compulsive e-mailing, cell-phoning, text-messaging, and facebooking. And although they can't articulate it, what many seem to be longing for is a place apart from the human-made world of technologies, ideas, and environs in which we have enclosed ourselves. Trapped inside our hall of mirrors, seeing only ourselves no matter which way we turn, we have all but lost sight of the larger sensuous world of non-human nature. From global warming to the oil-polluted Gulf of Mexico, we need only open the daily newspaper or turn on the six o'clock news to witness the devastating results.

The proper preparation and drinking of tea offer more than mere respite from this alienation. Not only is tea the Tao in disguise, it is also (as Toyohara Sumiaki writes in this book's epigraph) a *place* in disguise, *the hut beneath the pine*, or the hermitage of the Taoist sage recluse *in the midst of the city*. It is a retreat, a sanctuary where, for a brief period, you can shake off the dust of the world. Like the tea leaves in your bowl, you can reawaken to the larger flow of life and nature—not as separate from yourself, but as who and what *you have always been.* Realizing and then embodying this truth on ever-deeper levels is the beginning of sanity.

An avid proponent of the life-changing power of tea, the great tea master Sen no Rikyu said: "Imagine your life without tea. And if it's any different than it is now, you don't understand tea." The truth Rikyu is pointing to is subtle: over time, tea overflows into your life, whether you happen to be drinking it or not. The presence that is nurtured through a regular tea practice becomes indistinguishable from who and what you are. It goes without saying that, if tea can silently alter our way of being in the world, then it can also affect everyone and everything we come into contact with. Tea, like Tao, is a "way" (*Tao* means "way" or "path") that imperceptibly reawakens us to flow, to Being, and to our original nature.

> *Preparing tea, awareness becomes fine tuned.*
> *Drinking tea, presence becomes*
> *more and more refined.*
>
> *Over time, the relaxed alertness*
> *with which you raise the bowl to your lips*
> *pours into the rest of life as well.*
>
> *If during tea, why not all the time?*
> *Why not everywhere?*

Cha (tea) and Tao are intuitive and experiential. Always flowing, always changing, neither can be pinned down by conceptual language. To illustrate this, I've taken a small liberty with the first line of Lao-tzu's 2,500 year-old classic, the *Tao Te Ching,* by reinserting the word "Tea" for "Tao":

*"The (Tea) that can be talked about is not the real (Tea)."*

And yet, Lao-tzu scripted 5,000 characters attempting to talk about what can't be talked about, and the leaf and poetry have been sharing the same tea table for centuries.

That said, keep in mind that this small collection of poems is nothing more than a sign post that is meant to be chopped up and burned to boil water once you find the hut, shake off the world's dust and, sipping quietly apart from the deafening din, taste the larger Reality.

— *Daniel Skach-Mills*

## The Teahouse In Spring
*After Lu Tong*

I try—
but who can read when it's spring
and the tulip tree's in full bloom
across the water?

No contest!
the black-and-white pages in books
simply can't compete with all this color,
the fragrance that comes wafting in
when the tea server opens wide
the south wall's floor-to-ceiling row
of Ming latticework doors,
well! it's all I can do
not to leaf out myself
right here in this shaft of sunlight
sipping at my bowl of Jing Silver,
lifting us both into clouds,
into heaven.

# The Hut Beneath The Pine

*Eighteen Tea Poems*

*One*

The human world teaches people
how to compete, get noticed,
succeed.

Here in my little garden
success is whatever happens
to be blooming at the moment.
Renown: the full moon throwing
its shortlived silver spotlight
onto the pond.

Twenty years of so-called "education"
and just look at all the unlearning
I've had to do
in order to truly taste
this one bowl of tea.

*Two*

Nearly spring—
and what can compare
with this freedom rain has,
coming and going all day
without once deciding to do so?
The pussy willow's downy catkins
appearing effortlessly,
with or without my say-so,
at the tip of a branch.

How many bowls
of Silver Needles I've sipped
watching all this unfold
through the teahouse window,
I couldn't begin to tell you.

The more the years accrue,
the less knowing matters.

## Three

The time taken for tea
takes a lifetime.

How can this be so?

The first steeping is like youth:
potent, powerful, its brash strength
often leads to bitterness.

The second tastes of middle age:
flowing like Tao,
the flavor's mellow and balanced.
There's enough life left
in the leaves for more.

Like an old man or woman,
the third has lost its vigor—
the color's pale,
the Qi's weak.

Writing poetry, drinking tea,
people say I'm acting childish,
wasting my life, approaching old age
with nothing to show for it
just like joy-filled
Ch'eng Hao.

*Four*

The person awakened to the Tao
is like a good pot of tea—
strong, but not biting,
smooth, but not weak,
she brings people together,
permeates the entire room with fragrance
without even trying,
embodies the One Source that fills
an infinite variety of cups.

This is why people relax in her presence:
because she brings what's been
gathered on the heights
down to where people can taste it;
pours herself freely into emptiness,
which is why those around her
experience being filled.

Ask, and she'll tell you
her job is easy.
She simply lets whatever comes
brew into what it is.

*Five*

Already the fourth steeping.
One more infusion,
and these leaves will be spent.

How is it that this rendezvous
I have each day with tea leaves and water,
bubbling kettle and gaiwans
pours out and unfolds
so quickly?

When lovers are together
the time passes swiftly.
Apart, it hardly moves.

Pining away like this
until our next meeting,
is it any wonder that these bowls
I raise my lips to
are drunk with anything less
than love?

*Six*

Steam curlicues from the spout
of my silver tea kettle.
Sunlight, my only guest,
enters through the window
and takes a seat in the chair.

In a porcelain gaiwan,
white as mountain mist or cloud,
Jing Mai leaves reawaken
ten thousand miles
from where they began.

To a heart rooted in the Tao,
what difference does time
or distance make?

Sipping tea,
I taste the contentment
of not knowing what
my next move will be
until it moves.

## Seven

See distinctions,
but remain indistinct.
Use descriptions,
but remain nondescript.

The bowl can be emptied
of everything but emptiness.
The mind can be filled
with everything
but the Tao.

What is it like to be filled
with the Tao?

The sound of the lid
clicking into place
atop the porcelain tea bowl
reduces you to tears.

*Eight*

Tea leaves float in my blue-and-white gaiwan.
White clouds drift in the sky-blue bowl
of the pond.

Near water, everything takes time to reflect.
I pause, sip. A scrub jay stoops to drink.

Oversteeped in words,
how can the tongue ever hope to taste
the Oneness being poured
into and out of
who knows how many
different cups?

*Nine*

A tea set has many cups,
but only one pot.
The Tao has many followers,
but there is only one Tao.

As the cups are emptied,
the drink becomes the drinker.
As the person's emptied,
the follower becomes the followed.

Words like *become* and *many*,
*follower* and *followed*
all clog the one spout
of what it is I'm trying to say.

Just be the emptiness
you've always been
steeped in.

*Ten*

Those who are truly free
aren't identified with
their own thinking.

Those identified
with their own thinking
aren't truly free.

Opening fully to what is,
tea leaves free the water
to be more than just water.

Seeing through itself completely,
water frees the leaves to be more
than what they could be alone.

Being the silent empty cup
that allows all this to happen
is called: *offering others a taste
of what they truly are.*

*Eleven*

Don't call it multi-tasking,
this ritual I do: lifting, pouring,
setting the pot down again
and raising the bowl to my lips.

Stepping into the tearoom,
I shake off the dust of the world.
Rinsing off the teaware,
I wash away thoughts from my mind.

Retreating an hour
from the world of men,
the only "bottom line"
is the one you are reading right now.

*Twelve*

Sitting in the teahouse,
all the noise of the city
fades to the periphery.

Resting in the Tao,
all the mental noise
does the same.

Use the city when you need it.
Otherwise, remain in the teahouse.

Use thinking when you need it.
The rest of the time,
be like the silent open pot that waits,
never knowing which will be
the next flavor of tea.

*Thirteen*

There's no convincing water in a bucket
that there really is an ocean.
There's no illuminating sunlight
to a stone hidden in a cave.

The terms *fall, winter, spring*
hold no meaning for an insect
that lives and dies in summer.
Its life is bound to a single season.

What words can capture
the joy I feel sweeping the front stairs?
slicing celery? brewing a pot of tea?

How do you talk
about the Great Oneness
to a mind that's like a broom
always raising a cloud of dust?
a knife slicing everything in two?
a mesh screen straining life
through a thousand thoughts?

*Fourteen*

A split in the teahouse door lets in the chill.
A crack in my teapot's lid lets out the heat.

The more you drink from the Tao's oneness,
the less energy you'll waste trying
to keep some things in and others out.

Beyond the window, a sudden breeze sends
yellow katsura leaves fluttering onto Zither Lake.

## Fifteen

Tea isn't an idea.
Contemplate it all you want,
you have to sip it for yourself
to taste what it really is.

The Tao isn't a concept.
The more you forget
thinking about it,
the easier it is
to remember.

It's like this—
an old monk, ninety years old,
wonders: *why is it I can't remember
anything I learned in school,
but can still recall the first
dirty joke I ever heard?*

## Sixteen

Six years till sixty,
I do Tai Chi, brew my leaves,
have no time for nonsense.

The man who tells me
he's beside himself with worry
obviously isn't standing
far enough away.

If he were,
words like *self* and *worry*
would melt from his vocabulary
like snow in the sun.

He would be
like a placid mountain pool
that's completely at rest
in rough craggy places
others consider hard;
that holds ten thousand storms,
but doesn't resemble
a single one.

*Seventeen*

Windswept pines twisting like dragons
from misty seaside cliffs.
Sun rising over the coast range
like Shen Long's flaming pearl.

Far below this rippling green tide
of salt-sprayed headland forest, breakers crash.
Air in the shifting sand of my body
ebbs and flows like waves.
In rolling surf, I can hear
the ancient Taoists' Healing Breath.

Boiling on the surface,
but tranquil in the depths,
what better place than by the sea
to prepare my tea ocean with cups and pot?
To watch my steaming kettle
for crab-eye, fish-eye,
and old fisherman water.

*Eighteen*

Is the fish in the water,
or is the water in the fish?

Are you in the environment,
or is the environment in you?

Tea, when it cools,
becomes the temperature
of its surroundings.
Your body, when it dies,
will do the same.

You *are* the environment,
seeing, hearing, smelling,
touching, and tasting itself.

You are the tea you are drinking
before it ever reaches your lips.

## Synesthesia

The monastery bell tinges twilight
with the zested pitch of citron,
its tart reverb tingling my nose
with a rind's ringing scent.

Like stitch, like weave,
this note is the bell's metallic thread
brocading my flesh with timbre,
a sonorous sharp penetrating
the fir-needled
pincushions
of hills.

Within each pupil's ring of sight,
this peal is the feather-soft arrowhead
of southbound geese
piercing the sky's purple bruise of cloud—
its downpour of sound:
a tarnished weary silver.

On my tongue,
the tone resonates tea
tolling from an ancient bush
in the mountains
no one has ever found.

# Tea Trio

*After Fan Chengda*

*One*

Old men "Disputing for Tens" at the tea table in the corner.
Win, lose, they love what I love—the pot full.
The way things click, as effortlessly as tiles on wood
or lids on tea tins, between them.

*Two*

Black clouds raining against teashop windows.
White Dragon pouring from my cup's cloud-ragged rim.
Twenty years following Cha Tao, is there any tea to drink
    that isn't the world?
That doesn't pour itself out completely into whatever
    brokenness it finds?

*Three*

Fog scudding over the west hills.
Steam swirling off my pot's Yixing clay.
Separated only by heartbreak's countless miles, see how
I still sip the tea we used to share, savoring its one taste.

# Cha Tao

I came to tea late in life,
the age of rare puerh,
words like *gongfu* and *yixing*,
*gaiwan* and *bing cha*
unfolding their foreign flavors
onto the pointed leaf tip of my tongue.

I sip from teaware painted and glazed,
etched and fired, not with the grimace and claw
of western wyverns steeped in stolen treasure,
pots of hoarded gold
(Europe's fire-breathing smoke screen
for its own projections),
but with the auspiciously weighted scales
of Shen Long, China's lucky dragon,
the azure sky of his body
coiling fluid as steam,
a ribbon whipped at the end
of a child's stick
serpentining the cloud-white curve
of my tea bowl's lid,
its porcelain rim delicate
as a wren's sip,
sheer as light poured from
the moon's full-bellied pot
into this China we call *bone*—
fragile ancestor holding
this small body of water,
a lifetime of pouring out
and drinking in.

# Watching An Old Monk Drink Tea

There is no drinker.
That shallow cup was emptied
years ago.

Nothing left now but the rough,
hand-thrown mug
cradled precariously as prayer
between the crumbling clay of his palms,
the vessel that begins empty and ends empty
no matter how fast or slow he sips.

Bitterness, weakness,
sweetness when it happens
is just the vow he's steeped in,
his trembling lips raised
to the passing steam
of whatever life pours out,
the fragile handle he knows
we have on things
as chipped and cracked
as it ever was.

## On Retreat

Sun rising through the monastery window.
A single ray needling light through a thousand pines.
Before morning clears these fog-blanketed hills,
monks will be soughing Lauds.

On my desk,
the mug of tea is as cold as my pen.
The sheet of paper's blank.
Prayer, in these matters, doesn't help.
Poems arise, or they don't.

Wind blows through the trees at will,
but who can quote it
or its source?

## At The Hermitage

A chill wind blows through my tiny wood stove.
The last gust extinguishes it for the fourth time.
Embers at this late hour barely illumine the room.
In such scant light, don't we all let go of what
we thought we were looking for? Hopes.
Dreams. The second book of matches.
My aging hands measuring tea leaves in the dark,
letting whatever unfolds be enough.

## Observing An Elderly Couple
## Sipping Tea At A Table
## Outside The Teahouse
*Lan Su Chinese Garden – Portland, Oregon*

What dialog there is—
*Good? Yes. More? Yes—*
could be the rare single-syllabled bird
alighting briefly on the table between them,
their shared seasons of marital molt
reducing words to the finest dander,
the fledgling flap of the lips
preened meticulously into this furl
of feather-soft spokenness,
this single wingbeat
of silently navigated air.

In the flashing tail feathers
of this evening's light
his eyes are blue as robins' eggs,
her hair: a silver nest.

When they do speak,
it is with the effortless soar of knowing
each where the other will land
before either of them
arrives there.

## At The Pavilion For Washing Away Thoughts

*Liu Fang Yuan/The Garden of Flowing Fragrance –
San Marino, California*

Thinking outside the box?
Thinking *is* the box.

No time like the present?
The present has nothing to do with time.

The one truth you can believe?
That nothing you believe is ultimately true.

Meditation is like life—
the harder you try to force
something to happen or not happen
the more difficult both become.

Cha Tao is like life—
the way becomes a struggle
only when your mind thinks the tea
should taste different than it does.

The master has emptied her cup of all thoughts.
She has no argument with whatever life pours out.
Lovingly, serenely, she holds the world to her lips.
Sipping only what is, she ends every war.

## At The Teahouse
*Lan Su Chinese Garden – Portland, Oregon*

Inside, it's warm.
Infused with choices
I order Chrysanthemum Flower;
you, Jade Cloud.

Outside, mist drizzles softly
into the ornate cup of the garden,
steeps slowly into the green tea
of the pond.

Here, nothing is strained.
Together we sip, leisurely as clouds
from the pools of leaves and petals
floating in the gaiwan bowls—
lids, like our conversation, held back a bit
so as to filter what's superfluous
from our lips.

Behind us,
the two women
pouring out to one another
refill after refill,
water under the covered bridge
about their most recent breakups,
each of us cradling the warm
but fragile touch of porcelain
in our hands.

Beside them,
the little altar
with its sweet smell
of burned-out incense
lying in a heap of ashes
at the feet of Kuan Yin.

## Now That I Realize Inner And Outer Are One
*After reading Penelope Scambly Schott's*
*"Now That I Live Among the Baboons"*


The teahouse door squeaks with laughter at its own joke.
It opens the widest of loves to everything
I've failed to let in or out.

The teahouse door mocks my taking sides.
It centers itself squarely, again and again,
in the still quiet space prior to coming and going.
It unlocks all my dead-bolt beliefs in life
as push and pull.

A sign that reads *Turn Off Cell Phones, Please*
floats in its pool of clear glass.
No WIFI here, either.
No high speed anything.
Service is slow, the way tea flowing
from an Yixing spout is slow.

The door has no idea which side is other.
The dreams it swings into and out of are hingeless.

As unaware of tarnish as it is of its own shine,
see how the door's brass pull-ring
gives itself in marriage
to every extended hand.
How it weds us at its center
to the emptiness
that opens everything.

# Glossary/Notes

**Bing Cha** – tea that has been dried and pressed into a round wheel or cake.

**Cha Tao** – "the Way of tea."

**Ch'eng Hao** – a Chinese poet of the Sung dynasty who lived from 1032–1085. The references to "acting childish" and "wasting my life" are from his poem *Casual Poem on a Spring Day*, in which he states that, although people say these things about him, they cannot "see the joy in (his) heart."

**Crab-eye, fish-eye, old fisherman water** – tea masters visually gauge the water temperature as it begins to boil. The tiny bubbles, referred to as "crab eyes" appear first. "Fish eyes" come next and are definitely larger. "Old fisherman" is rapidly boiling water. Fish-eye water is preferred for most teas.

**"Disputing for Tens"** – also known as "Ts'ung Shap," a Chinese domino game.

**Fan Chengda** – (1126–1193) a poet of the Sung dynasty who was a master of the "cut short" or *jue ju* four-line form of Chinese verse.

**Gaiwan** – (pronounced "guy whan") a tea bowl with a saucer and lid.

**Gongfu** – translates as "art" or "skill." Gongfu tea is the art of preparing and presenting tea.

**Healing Breath** – as part of their Tai Chi practice, the ancient Taoists incorporated healing sounds which strengthened different organs in the body. Sounds such as *tzuh*, *shu*, *hsi*, and *shui* were often aspirated. As such, they resemble the sound of the surf.

**Jade Cloud** – a loose-leaf green tea.

**Jing Mai** – a loose-leaf white tea.

**Jing Silver** – a loose-leaf white tea.

**Kuan Yin** – the Chinese goddess/bodhisattva of compassion and mercy. She is often depicted holding a vase, from which she pours healing into the world; and a willow branch, symbolizing affectionate bonding and freedom from maladies.

**Lu Tong** – a poet of the Tang dynasty (618–907). His famous poem, *The Seven Bowls of Tea*, ends with the line: "Oh, the seventh cup, I'd better not drink it, or I'm off to heaven."

**Pavilion For Washing Away Thoughts** – a small, open-air, thatched-roof pavilion at *The Garden of Flowing Fragrance* in San Marino, California. Thatched-roof huts were traditionally the abodes of poets, hermits, and scholars. The name, "Washing Away Thoughts," comes from the story of the Chinese imperial official, Wu Yuanheng, who received a rare and prized tea from the emperor. The tale relates how tea can "wash away" the thoughts, cares, and concerns of a high-ranking official working within the imperial bureaucracy. It also reflects the Taoist principle of *Su*, or mental stillness and quietude.

**Puerh** – (pronounced "poo-are") a fermented black tea which typically comes in small chunks called "tea bricks." Puerh improves with age and, like fine wine, increases in value the older it gets. Health benefits associated with drinking puerh include lowering cholesterol and flushing plaque from the arteries.

**Qi** – (also spelled "chi," and pronounced "chee") the life force energy.

**Sen no Rikyu** – (1522–1592) the great Japanese tea master who taught the four merits of tea: humility, purity, harmony, and respect.

**Shen Long's flaming pearl** – the Chinese dragon, Shen Long, exhales the cosmic life force which is often depicted in Chinese art as a flaming pearl.

**Silver Needles** – loose-leaf white teas.

**Synesthesia** – a momentary exchange or fusion of the senses. A common phenomenon in Taoism and some schools of Buddhism, synesthesia is often precipitated by reading or writing poetry, especially Taoist poetry.

**Tai Chi** – a Chinese form of exercise characterized by slow rhythmic movements that mimic the movements in nature, especially the flow of water. Tai Chi practice facilitates good health by keeping the energy pathways (or "meridians" as they're called in Chinese medicine) in the body open so that the Qi can move freely.

**Tao** – (pronounced "Dow." Sometimes spelled "Dao.") translates as "way" or "path." Some scholars speculate that Taoism's roots go back to ancient shamanism in China (ca. 7000 BCE). In the 6th century BCE, someone (reputedly named Lao-tzu) wrote and/or compiled from various oral sources a manual on the art of living entitled, the *Tao Te Ching*, or *The Book of the Virtue of the Way*. Despite all that has been said and written about it, Tao cannot be named or conceptualized. As such, it is the "way" we forge beyond intellectual knowledge. To ask "what is it?" is to have already missed it. Tao isn't a "what" or an "it." We could say, "Tao is," but this, too, misses the mark as Tao is beyond and prior to opposites like *is* and *isn't*. More verb than noun, it is present as the intelligent, rhythmic flow of nature that we witness both around and within us. Hills flow, as do coastlines, clouds, tree branches, and water. Everything flows. Even our breathing flows in and out like the ocean waves.

**Tea ocean** – a bowl (usually porcelain or Yixing clay) which the pot and cups are placed into for rinsing and heating with hot water.

**Water in a bucket/an insect that lives and dies in summer** – these images were inspired by the teachings of Chuang-tzu (ca. 369 – ca. 286 BCE).

**White Dragon** – a loose-leaf white tea.

**Wyvern** – a two-legged dragon with wings, two small arms, and a barbed and knotted tail. The dragon on the Welsh flag is a wyvern.

**Yixing** – (pronounced "ee-shing") teaware from the Yixing region in eastern China. Also called "Purple Sand" or "Purple Clay" teaware, Yixing originated during the Sung dynasty (960–1279), and is most often used to prepare oolong and puerh teas. The porous clay absorbs the tea flavor with continued usage. It's said that a well-used Yixing teapot can brew tea without using any leaves.

**Zither Lake** – the poetic name of the lake at Lan Su Chinese Garden in Portland, Oregon.

# About the Author

Daniel Skach-Mills was born in Coeur d'Alene, Idaho, and raised in Portland, Oregon. He holds an undergraduate degree from Marylhurst University, Marylhurst, Oregon; and a graduate degree from St. Martin's University in Lacey, Washington. His award-winning poetry has been published in a variety of publications and anthologies, including: *The Christian Science Monitor*; *The Christian Century*; *Sojourners*; *Open Spaces*; and *Prayers To Protest: Poems That Center And Bless Us* (Pudding House Publications, 1998). His chapbook, *Gold: Daniel Skach-Mills's Greatest Hits, 1990–2000* was published by Pudding House in 2001; and a full-length collection, *The Tao of Now*, (published by Ken Arnold Books in 2008) was listed as one of the "150 outstanding Oregon poetry books" by Jeff Baker, columnist for *The Oregonian*; David Biespiel, editor of *Poetry Northwest*; and Jim Scheppke, Oregon State Librarian.

He has been a featured reader in the northwest for events at Barnes and Noble (Vancouver, WA); Looking Glass Bookstore; Marylhurst University; Lan Su Chinese Garden; Living Earth Gatherings; KBOO Radio; Blackbird Wine Bar; Moonstruck Chocolate Café; The Q Center; Broadway Books; The Tenth Muse Books (Seaside); Rilassi Coffee House; The Hundredth Monkey Art Studio; Nritya Mandala Mahavihara Newari Buddhist Temple; The Milwaukie Poetry Series; and The Friends of William Stafford.

A volunteer docent for Lan Su Chinese Garden since 2005, Daniel was invited to Mexico City, Mexico in 2009 to give a two-day presentation on Classical Chinese Gardens and Taoism. He has lived both as a Benedictine and a Trappist monk, and currently resides with his partner in Portland, Oregon.

7724653R0

Made in the USA
Charleston, SC
03 April 2011